OUTDOOR LIVING

OUTDOOR LIVING

Courtyards, Decks and Patios

Edited by Andrea Boekel

images
Publishing

Published in Australia in 2007 by
The Images Publishing Group Pty Ltd
ABN 89 059 734 431
6 Bastow Place, Mulgrave, Victoria 3170, Australia
Tel: +61 3 9561 5544 Fax: +61 3 9561 4860
books@images.com.au
www.imagespublishing.com

National Library of Australia Cataloguing-in-Publication entry:

Outdoor Living – Courtyards, Decks and Patios

ISBN 1 876907 55 X.

1. Outdoor living spaces. 2. Patios. 3 Pergolas. 4. Courtyards

728.93

Edited by Andrea Boekel

Designed by The Graphic Image Studio Pty Ltd, Mulgrave, Australia
www.tgis.com.au

Digital production by Splitting Image Colour Studio Pty Ltd, Australia
Printed by Sing Cheong Printing Co. Ltd. Hong Kong

IMAGES has included on its website a page for special notices in relation to this
and our other publications. Please visit www.imagespublishing.com

Contents

Contents (continued)

Introduction

Outdoor living spaces have been an important architectural feature for thousands of years. The earliest civilisations in central Asia, China and North Africa all incorporated courtyards in their building schemes.

Long associated with calm, stillness, security and tranquillity, even today amidst mounting urban growth, courtyards, patios, decks, gazebos and pergolas nurture the feeling of serenity and solitude.

Just as the ancient Persians regarded courtyards as miniature replicas of heaven, we also derive much pleasure from outdoor living spaces. They heighten sensory perception: smell is stimulated by blooming flowers or a summer rain; sight is drawn to a still pond or a green oasis of tropical plants; while hearing tunes into the incessant gurgling of a water feature, the call of a bird or the meditative drone of crickets and frogs.

Outdoor living spaces often change the entire way inhabitants regard their homes. They can be adapted to almost any large or small space where they can be adorned with foliage, stone, water and light, as they become true extensions of a home as well as the intermediary between indoors and outdoors. They can be entertainment areas, places for afternoon siestas and personal retreat. Heating and fire pits incorporated into the design enable year-round use of these courtyards, patios and decks, even on chilly nights.

The projects within this book have been carefully chosen for their diverse characteristics. There are classic courtyards like House + House Architects' Casa des Estrellas in Mexico, which feature elements like terracotta, wrought iron and mosaic and Neo-Classical outdoor spaces like MBH Architecture's Newport Coast Villas with water fountains and statues of cherubs and mythical horses. But it does not end there. Studio Gaia's private penthouse atop a metropolitan New York building provides a restful area and escape from the whirl of city life. The landscaped gardens of Marcelo Novaes Paisagismo in Brazil, the primitive outdoor 'quinchos' of Argentina by Rafael Iglesia, Praachi Design's mogul-inspired courtyard in New Delhi full of brilliant colour and romance and Jeffrey Gordon Smith Landscape Architecture's whimsical courtyards in California portray the many faces of today's outdoor living spaces.

This book aims to return a little bit of heaven into the reader's life. For many, these outdoor spaces will recall reminiscences of special evenings spent in cherished amity with friends and family. They evoke peace, inspiration and harmony. The projects featured in this book endeavour to take the reader through outdoor havens where even more treasured memories will be inspired.

Andrea Boekel
Editor

Projects

House for Two Architects

This residence was once an unpretentious hacienda in the centre of a village with cobbled streets and bougainvillaea-draped walls. Over the centuries, the land was fragmented and eventually all that was left was the back door and a few storage sheds on a small property. The architects commenced remodelling the remnants: a beautiful old door that led to the remaining structures on a piece of land 11 metres by 16 metres.

The main living spaces open onto and flow through the central courtyard, with guest quarters and studio space on the second floor. An array of balconies and terraces give the impression of a complete little village.

Traditional Mexican hues of salmon, ochre and deep red are lime washes, each glowing with natural light at different times of the day. Ochre river rock and hand-quarried slate swirl together in the courtyard paving. Original materials blend with traditional details in this contemporary home.

Photography: Steven House

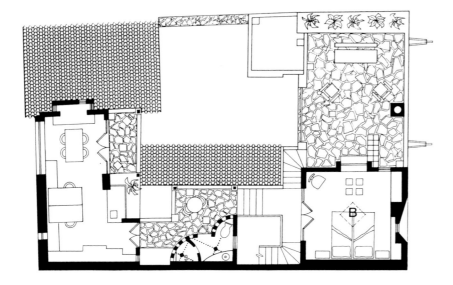

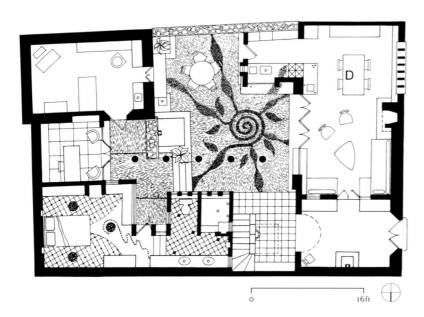

0   16ft

Walski Residence

Water and outdoor living are the main themes for this house. The entry gate has water flowing on both surfaces of rippled glass. It opens onto a spacious courtyard paved with flagstones and a reflecting pool.

The courtyard also works as a pre-function space for special occasions. The residence integrates the outside with the inside by boldly continuing natural elements indoors. Water playfully flows from the roof into a seemingly overflowing pool.

Presenting spectacular views of the Santa Rosa Mountains, the patio welcomes the desert landscape with its large outcropping of boulders that surround the pool. All living spaces are designed to have a seamless connection between indoors and outdoors. When all the pocket doors are open, the house seems to recede into the background as the sculptural desert landscape comes into focus.

Photography: David Glomb

Patel Architecture/Narendra Patel, AIA

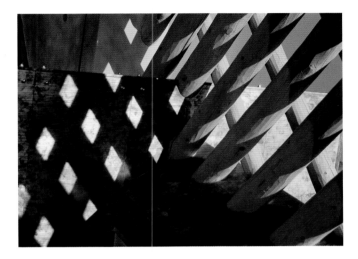

Olivium Villas

Studio Alhadeff Architects

Olivium Villas present the blending of modern Mediterranean style with international flair. They combine minimalist dimensions with warm materials. A vacation development, the houses are positioned to complement the natural environment and accentuate the dramatic play of mountain, sea and sky. No two houses are alike and no two vistas are the same. Positioned to make optimum use of existing mature olive trees and other flora, the site's challenges of gradient also add to the design scheme.

The outdoor spaces create a coherent interplay of stucco and stone, mountain and sky, hillside and waterscape. Terraced living spaces inspire the unusual positioning of pools and courtyards; indoor and outdoor living areas that challenge the normal layout of living on different levels.

Photography: Yavuz Draman/Drogan Burda

Pathak House

The bold and vibrant style of the courtyard and terrace of this house uses solid areas of dazzling colour to give a sense of space and depth. Because the courtyards are sprinkled within the house, the entire house glows with warmth and colour whatever the climate is outside. The sun streams through the courts and makes interesting patterns of light and shade throughout the day.

The terrace canopy surrounded by greenery is the most utilised space. It is an ideal space for the family to gather and enjoy the evening breezes or watch a monsoon shower while relishing hot tea. Indian-inspired vermilion hues and mirrors typical of the nomadic mud houses of Kutch in the state of Gujrat adorn this space.

The terrace is a cool, uncluttered space achieved by the minimal use of ornamentation. A spare turquoise blue urn and a dry tree with wind chimes hanging from its branches provide a sense of tranquil calm.

Both courtyards are strategically placed and form an extension from the living and dining spaces. Comfortable floor seating with hand embroidered and mirrored cushions in jewel colours add to the romantic feel. Ultramarine blue, emerald green and turquoise lend depth to this courtyard where planters and plantings echo the same colour scheme.

Photography: Taj Mohammed

Praachi Design Pvt. Ltd.

700 Palms Residence Courtyard

Steven Ehrlich Architects

This residence is situated on the corner of a street of traditional beach bungalows, lined with palms. Three distinct courtyards grace the compound, which is designed for large family gatherings and overnight guests.

The first, the main courtyard, lies between the main house and the guesthouse. Artist Woods Davey set free-form granite in ornamental grass. A raised patio for alfresco meals creates multi-use spaces that fully exploit the benign climate. Through pivoting two-storey glass-and-metal doors, the kitchen and main living area opens up to the main courtyard. An 80-year-old canary palm also serves as a focal point to the main courtyard.

A lap pool on the west is situated within another courtyard with the main entrance to the home. Sliding glass doors open the living area fully to the west courtyard. The north courtyard exposes the living area through pocketing glass doors, to an 80-year-old Aleppo pine.

The courtyards within the premises are each starkly different in design and component. The courtyards blend with the raw, honest materials appropriate to the bohemian grittiness of Venice and dissolve the barriers between indoors and out.

Photography: Erhard Pfeiffer

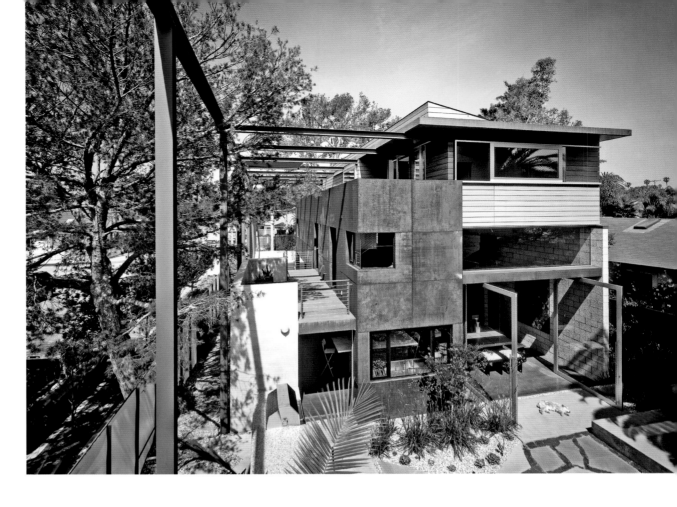

Quincha

Rafael Iglesia Arquitectos

This miniscule structure is a traditional 'quincho' or 'eating place'. The design scheme is simple: a couple of porous walls, a roof and a table. Despite this fact, it is also a place for meditation and reflection, elevating the small shelter beyond its function. A swimming pool is situated alongside the structure.

The most obvious relationship to nature is the tree trunk supporting the flat roof. This design reaches back to the roots of architecture, the primordial hut. This column sits next to the earthen hearth that also acts as a third 'wall' for the eating enclosure.

As alluded to, the quincho is an enclosure designed deliberately with the sun and with nature in mind. The sun entering through gaps in the porous wood walls creates shadows across the wood floor and the glints on the water reflect on the ceiling.

Photography: Gustavo Frittegotto

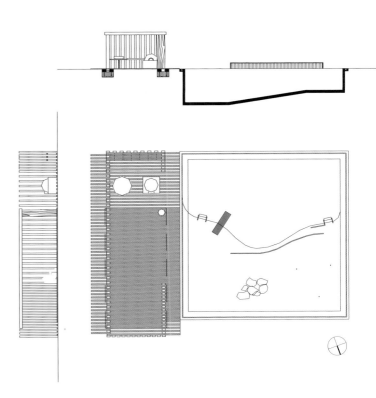

Woll Residence

SAN LUIS OBISPO, CALIFORNIA, USA

Jeffrey Gordon Smith Landscape Architecture

A tall vertical water feature is the main focal point of the outdoor spaces of this residence. The fountain is constructed with a corrugated concrete column that falls into a triangular basin that doubles as a raised drinking basin for the clients' dogs. The ground plan is designed with a herringbone-patterned ipe deck that invites one to enter the next outdoor room. A large pergola is incorporated as the outdoor kitchen that embraces the Kamado barbecue.

Interweaving fingers of a pre-cast concrete sidebar grasp the pergola post while custom-made storage cabinets on castors become serving side tables. The next room incorporates a built-in spa dropped below the deck level that is surrounded and disguised by a raised bench. Adjacent to this room lies an outdoor gas fire pit constructed with a concrete basin filled with recycled glass. Each of these rooms is set on a 45-degree angle and surrounded by layers of plants creating a stunning backdrop that keeps the eye away from the close property line.

Photography: Elliot Johnson

Bottger House

Hugo Hamity Architects

Access to this existing single-storey, 1970s residence, is through a courtyard that announces the arrival and the change of frequency from exterior to interior activities. The courtyard is divided into two by a water feature garden that also serves as a storm water drain. The existing 35-year-old terracotta tiles were retained and integrated with the new structural elements.

Outside, the existing garden is divided into open courtyards with different functions expressed in a flexible and open manner. Varying in formality of design and realisation, they are skilfully integrated into the new structures through the conservation of the original open patio paving patterns.

Photography: Karin Brady

Bratton Residence Courtyard

LOS ALTOS, CALIFORNIA, USA

House + House Architects/Cathi House

An addition and renovation transformed this 1950s suburban house into an elegant, contemporary home of light-filled spaces around a sunny, entry courtyard.

A raised concrete path leads through the courtyard, and forms a bridge across a reflecting pool. The embracing glass walls amplify the splashing sounds and ripples of water that shimmer over the stainless steel fountain.

A bed of river rock is the base for a steel sculpture from a local artist and provides a soft bed for the still waters of the pool. The skewed, slatted wood contemplation bench invites momentary pause in the sun. A timeless elegance binds the interior with the exterior and blends the traditional and contemporary with ease.

Photography: Mark Luthringer

Desert House

Marmol Radziner & Associates

Located on a five-acre site, this prototype prefab home is orientated to capture the stunning views of San Jacinto peak and the surrounding mountains.

The house extends through the landscape with covered outdoor living areas, which double the interior spaces of the 185-square-metre house. Sheltered living spaces blend the indoors with the outdoors, simultaneously extending and connecting the house to the north wing.

By forming an "L" shape, the home creates a protected courtyard environment that includes a pool and fire pit. The courtyard provides relaxing spaces to enjoy the surrounding open environment. The furniture including the chaise lounges and the fire pit benches were custom designed by the architects to complement the modern aesthetic of the architecture and the rustic beauty of the desert surrounds.

Photography: David Glomb, Benny Chan/Fotoworks

Alta

The butterfly roof, an asymmetrical cantilever that reinforces the sense of orientation, opens up to maximise views of the surrounding mountains and sky. From the outside, this roof appears to float over the house giving it an indoor/outdoor pavilion character.

The kitchen and dining rooms open to the front and back courtyards. Zen-type settings provide a quiet and tranquil recess. The master suite also opens up to the courtyard and Zen garden.

The courtyard serves as a centrepiece while the sinuous lines of the pool serve as an invitation to experience the space. The sun brings an ever-changing drama of light and shadow into the courtyard during the day. At twilight, the courtyard transforms into a glamorous backdrop as the entire interior of the house comes alive with low-voltage lighting design. The front gate and garden walls also let in light so that one feels enveloped but not contained. The courtyard is designed to promote a three-dimensional reflection of the inner landscape of a settled mind.

Photography: Arthur Coleman

Patel Architecture/Narendra Patel, AIA

Solar Box

Driendl Architects*

This private house, located in the 19th district of Vienna, was built at the beginning of the 20th century. At more than 80 years old, the relationship between house and garden was incompatible. Being also narrow and poorly lit, it was therefore necessary to gain both space and light when the extension was added.

The structure sits on a long and narrow north-orientated hilly site. An annexe was added onto the south side, with a large patio facing the garden. The south façade of the house was completely removed and the old building was stabilised with a steel frame.

Cheerful outdoor spaces for relaxing and enjoying the sunshine were created. A new 8-metre cube was erected in front of the new opened skin. The cube has been constructed using wood and glass to ensure sunlight penetrates while offering a view of the old building through the garden.

An open and airy terrace was created on top of this cube heightening the feeling of merging the outdoors with the indoors while the atrium-like feel of this structure adds to the interface between old and new.

Photography: Lew Rodin

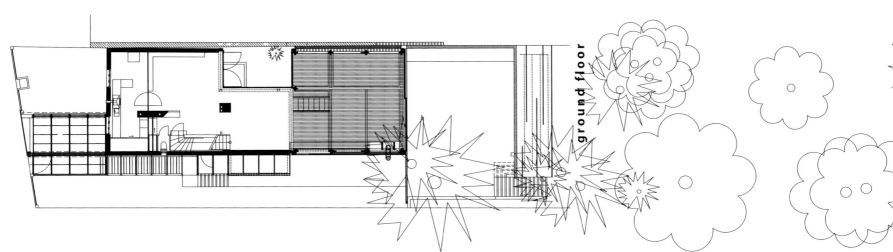

ground floor

Ward Residence

Marmol Radziner & Associates

Located in Rustic Canyon, one of the most serene areas of Los Angeles, this 1200-square metre home is effectively divided into two domains. A public pavilion includes the kitchen, living room and dining areas and a private pavilion contains the bedrooms. A glass-enclosed walkway that takes optimal advantage of the surrounding landscape connects the two areas.

Exits from the master bedroom and living room lead to a rear outdoor living area, which includes two extended patios and a simple yet elegant lap pool along the back of the property.

The garage serves as the foundation for the public pavilion whose front end juts out of the hillside, establishing a vertical connection to the foundations below.

Photography: Benny Chan/Fotoworks

Francisci Residence

Studio Alhadeff

This residence was once an oil press typical of the Umbrian landscape. It has been totally restored resulting in the re-opening of dramatic, double-height spaces visible from the entrance. It also commands spectacular views from within.

The original structure was expanded by the transformation of stables on the downhill side into additional guest bedrooms and the addition of a portico. Made of local stone, this portico extends over the upper living space and provides a lovely area to dine al fresco. A large open deck opens out from the portico and offers magnificent views over the surrounding olive groves.

Every attempt was made throughout the renovation phases to protect the surrounding trees and plants – typically mulberry and olive trees and to preserve the original feel of the structure within its rural setting. In the same spirit, traditional local materials such as handmade terracotta tiles, limestone and chestnut wood have been used. The predominant use of large limestone slabs for floors, walkways and stairs enhances the visual continuity of the interior and exterior living spaces.

Photography: Yavuz Draman/Drogan Burda

Casa Montaña

Daniel Perez-Gil Arquitectos

This multi-level residence is located on a mountain slope and consists of three main and two additional levels. It offers spectacular views of the nearby mountain landscape.

A high-tech and futuristic feel is achieved with a concrete structure crowned by a curved roof with a crystal dome, and walls of the same material. Main access is on ground level and mirrored water features adorn the entry. An outdoor terrace is also located on this level.

The central patio is the focal point of this house; it sits on an elevated height crowned by a crystal dome that filters sunlight and controls temperature. The entertainment and relaxation spaces, including the swimming pool and tennis court, are on a lower level. In all, the concept of merging indoors and outdoors is achieved in a lightweight and transparent manner.

Photography: Hector Armando Herrera

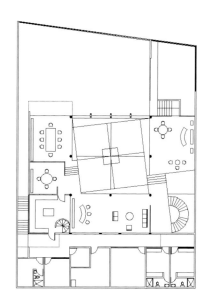

Nieto Residence

This award-winning residence retains the original craftsman-style beauty through material improvements and a natural, yet symmetrical planting design to further accent the home.

The designed landscape offers further support with typical craftsman-era details such as dry stacked walls, strong horizontal lines and rambling, natural plants.

In the backyard, concentric rings of *aloe striata*, *dymondia margaretae*, *cerastium tomentosum*, *senecio serpens* and *lotus maculatus* mimic rippling water. This echoes the design of the water feature that cascades the entire length of the garden to terminate in a semi-circle, and becomes a pleasant view from the master bedroom.

Photography: Elliot Johnson

Jeffrey Gordon Smith Landscape Architecture

Porter Residence

Studio 9 Architects

The contrast between the existing structure and the new open-plan addition lies in the distinction between the enclosed rooms of the Federation-style house and the open indoor/outdoor living areas that brim over with light and transparency.

The new works were designed from inside to out. The north light from high-level windows permits winter sun to penetrate while the fireplace reaches into the yard and the café-style folding doors provide the physical link to the veranda and outdoors.

The veranda can be used as a winter play area for children. The red stained concrete features both internally and externally and provides warmth and vibrancy to the overall design scheme.

Photography: Sarah Long Photography

Kent Residence

RANCHO MIRAGE, CALIFORNIA, USA

Patel Architecture/Narendra Patel, AIA

This lavish contemporary estate, with a touch of the Mediterranean, is designed for outdoor living and entertainment. The dramatic outdoor living areas consist of a multi-level pool and spa. Waterfalls, raised marble-covered planters and spacious patios create the sounds and feel of a magical retreat.

The guesthouse and pavilion has kitchen amenities and is perfect for outdoor entertainment. The pavilion includes two guest bedrooms, an outdoor kitchen and lavish patios. An overhang keeps out the hot desert sun during summer months and allows sunshine in during winter months. It allows the sun's rays to reflect on the pool and throw glints back up on the multi-levelled ceiling.

The constantly changing colour and direction of the sunlight, along with textured planes and well-defined edges, offer a special architectural element: natural light murals that shift from hour to hour and season to season.

Photography: Mark Knight, Nicola Pira

Glencoe Residence

Marmol Radziner & Associates

Responding to the surrounding context and lot sizes, this residence is a stepped two-storey house. Exterior connections between the ground floor living areas flanked by a garden running the length of the narrow lot maximise the available land.

The landscape was designed in conjunction with the architecture and creates a series of outdoor rooms that function seamlessly with the interior spaces to accommodate an indoor/outdoor lifestyle. The outdoor spaces, created by bisecting the garden into front and rear yards and the hidden entry gate, serve as the front door for both house and garden.

An outdoor dining room acts as the element that bridges the indoor and outdoor rooms. Connected to the main house, this dining area provides a transition between the passive front garden and more active rear garden. The swimming pool is the focus of the rear garden. Its rectangle of blue water echoes the rectangle of green lawn in the front.

Photography: Benny Chan/Fotoworks

Arrayan Lodge

Arquitectura Amoroso

'Arrayan' which means 'where the rays of the setting sun fall' in Mapuche, the Argentine aboriginal language, was so named by the owner as a tribute to the breathtaking beauty of this region. Built on a hill, facing the Lacar Lake and framed by the majestic Andean Cordillera in the distance, the lodge has a spectacular, panoramic view over the lake and the Andes.

This lodge has been designed keeping history and traditional local architecture in mind and its rustic and earthy character fits with the untamed nature of the site. The outdoor spaces take advantage of the stunning lake views. A wooden deck at the lower level overlooks the lake and has outdoor seating. Another wooden deck and an octagonal structure with an outdoor terrace on the upper level afford an unsurpassed view of mountain and lake.

Throughout the house, the rustic materials used such as stone and wood heightens the feeling of oneness with nature and embraces the pure countryside of this mountainous region.

Photography: Eliséo Miciu

Villa Deys

Architectenbureau Paul de Ruiter B.V.

The owners of Villa Deys specifically requested that the design for their house include a pool to help maintain their fitness in their older years. The result is a house that has been built around a pool, making it the building's connecting element.

Height similarities and a lack of thresholds seamlessly tie each spatial element in the programme. Even the water level of the swimming pool is as high as the floor. Every possible adaptation to the house has been made with the owners' age taken into account. From the sunscreens and sliding doors to the front door and even the curtains, almost everything can be controlled remotely.

Designed as two long volumes, the villa also has a lower-level volume in between where the swimming pool is located. The difference in height between the three volumes permits extra daylight to enter the building. The patio area is airy and spacious and projects a feeling of total serenity.

Photography: Alessio Guarina, Rien Van Rijthoven, René de Wit

Casa Vertientes

Pascal Arquitectos

This triple-level house combines timeless design with contemporary style. The outdoor spaces consist of neatly laid-out gardens with classic ornamentation such as a birdbath, arches and symmetrical plant beds.

The main entrance is located on the centre level. Classic styling with wooden floors, Greek marble columns, and Byzantine mosaics combined with classical furniture create a feeling of sophistication and warmth. This ambience is echoed even in the outdoors areas.

Photography: Jaime Navarro

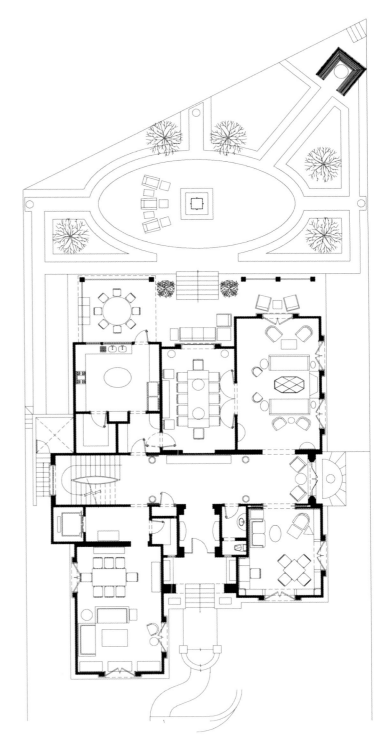

House in Yayoidai

Satoshi Okada architects

This house is located on a hill, in a suburb of Yokohama, close to Tokyo. The site was spare and also subject to local planning laws that limit structures to a maximum of two storeys, resulting in many nearby houses having basements.

The architect opposed the idea of an enclosed underground space, so courtyards were incorporated into the design. Two courtyards, the smaller one on the north and the larger on the south, induced natural sunlight and ventilation through an ingenious process of gravity and air.

When the air of the south courtyard is heated, it rises upwards. Because of this movement, the air in the north-side courtyard is forced to flow to the south side providing natural ventilation for the basement.

Photography: Satoshi Okada architects

Frye Residence

An addition and renovation transformed this home into a spacious and contemporary dwelling. A deep-set door of thick pine timber laced into a wooden grid invites entry through a garden.

The outdoor spaces are cool and restful and consist of several outdoor nooks. A rear garden and courtyard are planted with fruit trees and adorned by a garden sculpture. The courtyard paved in terracotta tiles has seating for outdoor meals with a fireplace for added warmth. A sculpted stairway off the courtyard leads to the upper floor.

Mexican tile flooring and integrally coloured concrete form the material palette in typical colours of russet, ochre and plum.

Photography: Steven House

House + House Architects/Cathi House

Erasmus House

Hugo Hamity Architects

This new home is located on a dolomite site filled with indigenous trees in a residential estate in Midrand. The aim of the design was to maximise the open, public areas while keeping the street relationship intact.

The outdoor living spaces make use of different materials and textures with nature and transparency the focus. The entry is announced by a shift on the focal point to the left and is adorned by a natural stone water feature. An indigenous, landscaped, water entrance atrium separates the vehicular access from the pedestrian. The use of a water feature at the entrance has a dual purpose, both as a decorative feature and as a means to reduce noise levels from the street.

An outdoor swimming pool acts as a definer between the garden and the interior. The rooms open out on to the wooden deck abutting the swimming pool and are sheltered by the cantilevered balconies above.

Photography: Karin Brady

Skrudás

Studio Granda

Skrudás is a family residence located in a new neighbourhood of Gardabaer, one of Reykjavik's satellite towns. The site is gently sloping on the northern side of a peninsula with an unbroken view of the Atlantic Ocean and Reykjavik with its magnificent mountain girdle. On the landside, suburbia closes in and one may say that the resultant tension between the closeness of neighbours and the uncluttered expanse of view is the principal generator of the design.

The house is approached from the south and is predominantly cuboid with a notched corner to indicate the entrance. On the garden side the external form is folded into itself to create a sheltered court.

The house is on three split-levels. On the mid level, the family room has large sliding doors that allow this space to extend into the court. An external stair leads from this court to a terrace shared by the dining, kitchen and living rooms. From this level, a long, stepped ramp leads to a large terrace and garden above the garage and *au-pair* flat. This grand external space is on the upper level and is sheltered from overview and wind by a shoulder-height wall enjoying both a close conversation with the garden court and long views out to sea.

Photography: Sigurgeir Sigurjónsson

Residence in the Bush

Marcelo Novaes Paisagismo

This residence is situated on a site that was once a forest on the outskirts of the sprawling city of São Paulo. The multi-level gardens still have many of the ancient towering trees that once existed, which provide much shade and coolness.

A covered patio and a lovely swimming pool also form the exterior living spaces. Unlike many residential swimming pools that are located away from trees because of the constant leaf fall, tall trees shade this pool and the atmosphere is cool and restful.

The garden slopes downwards from the residence. The entry garden is planted with tall palms and varieties of bromeliad and bamboo provide added interest. Crimson-coloured dwarf ixoras line the sides of the descending steps.

A covered patio area overlooks the pool and is a good area for entertaining. In another area of the garden, an additional seating area of eucalyptus logs on a bed of gravel adds a whimsical touch to the overall design scheme. A wide variety of tropical foliage and blooming plants such as ginger, heliconia, spathiphyllum, mussanda, plumbago and philodendron create the feel of a lush, tropical forest.

Photography: Gustavo Olmos

Minarc House

Minarc

The two architects who own this house are originally from Iceland. They transformed this post-World War II Californian bungalow into a modern home that seamlessly blends technology with a relaxed atmosphere within a very internationally styled space.

The outdoor spaces consist of a private garden and an open dining room that are separated from the indoor space by three wide, sliding glass door panels. When fully opened these act as a disappearing wall and unify the outdoors with the open floor plan.

The outdoor dining room has a heated wooden floor and additional ceiling heaters for cold, winter nights. Embodying the fusion of today's technology and the use of environmentally sensitive materials, the spaces are harmoniously joined with the intent of creating a fluid journey from indoors to outdoors. The result is a peaceful environment that reflects the modern ideologies of a family living in the midst of a complex urban setting.

Photography: Ralf Seeburger

Tradition-inspired Jordanian House
DEAD SEA, JORDAN

Ammar Khammash Architects

This unique house is located at the lowest point on earth, Jordan's Dead Sea basin. Every element of the house is unique, from the design to the construction, because it embodies the traditional Jordanian dwelling. The rapid growth of Jordan's capital city, Amman, has made access to the Dead Sea area relatively easy and the owners found themselves spending a lot of time in their vacation home. With a view of the Dead Sea from the south and the silhouette of Jerusalem from the west, the house acts as a viewing platform towards these vistas.

The relationship between indoors and outdoors is paramount; the house virtually lives with the landscape. Composed of several small spaces as opposed to one large structure it provides a variation between the vertical and horizontal elements. All the structures are made of locally quarried stone. A large, raised pond at the rear of the house, with a large surrounding patio, creates an area of cool recess. Stepped terraces that lead down to the lower level of the site recall ancient building techniques. Paved paths of stone meander throughout the outdoor spaces and the feel is that of a beautiful, traditional house easing in effortlessly with modern lifestyles.

Photography: Ammar Khammash

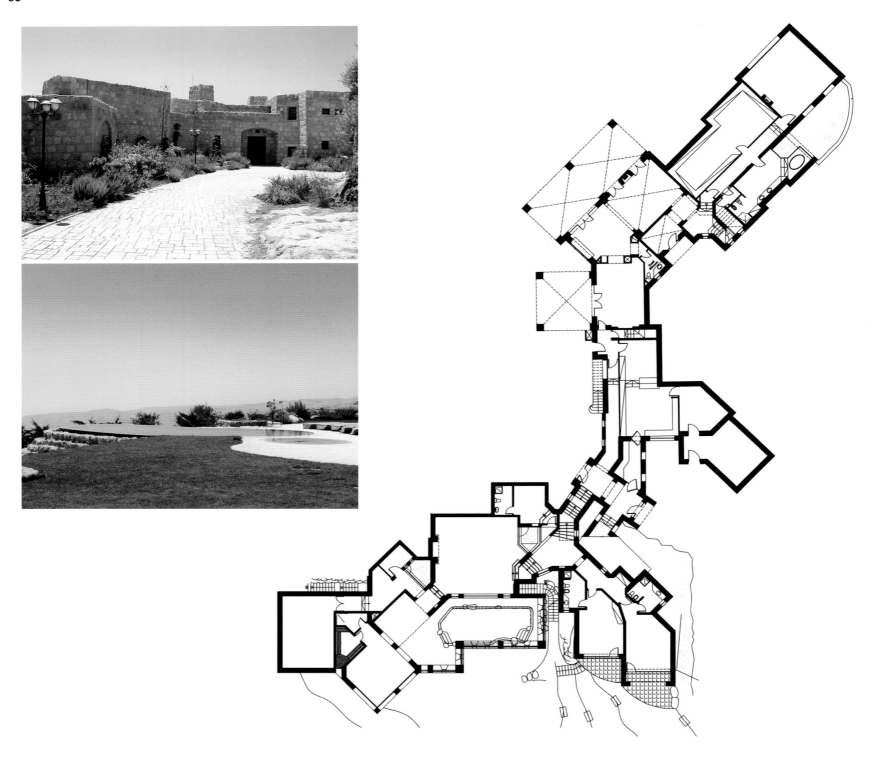

House in Aobadai

Satoshi Okada architects

Located on the Daikanyama Hill adjoining the fashionable Shibuya district of Tokyo, the house sits on a sloping, trapezoid-shaped site. The house is composed of two structural elements: one, reinforced concrete walls and slabs; the other, an iron-structured flat roof. A four-car garage on ground level occupies half of the site; the owner being a car-enthusiast.

On the first floor, the living section is sandwiched by two terraces. The large terrace above the garage doubles as an entertainment area and an outdoor bathing area. Along the north wall, a shallow, slow water stream with a green glass bottom filters the sunlight into the garage below and casts water shadows of its wall in the dark. The rear terrace provides more intimate and cosy ambience in contrast to the vibrant front terrace.

The bathroom and laundry is located on the ground floor along the south-end wall and the bathroom opens onto a tiny garden. This open space has a dual purpose functioning as a lightwell and ventilator and connecting to the master bedroom.

Photography: Satoshi Okada architects

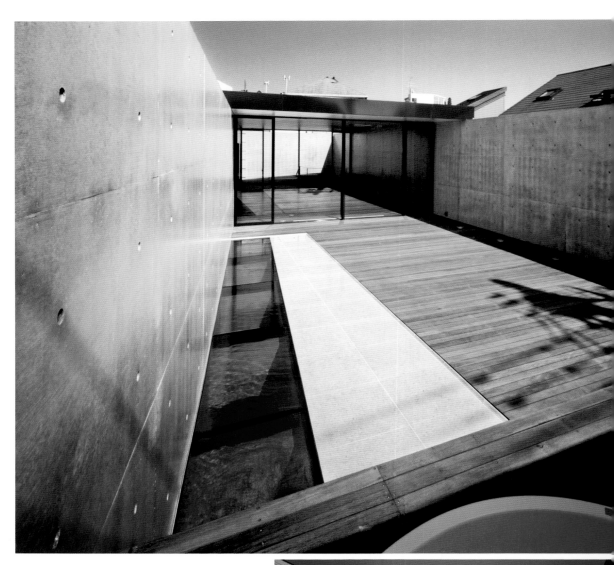

Newport Coast Villas

MBH Architects

Modelled on an Italian hillside village, this design concept involved recreating the village atmosphere of the Tuscany region in northern Italy. The ambience of this region was achieved with landscaping, stone paving, fountains and a grand piazza featuring a campanile structure.

The exterior living spaces include villas clustered around a central piazza with fountains, cascading pools, sculpture and numerous convenience shops. The use of historic materials such as plaster, ceramic tiles, clay roof tiles and wood trellises evoke the images of Tuscany.

The project is set in a thriving landscape of olive and palm trees overlooking neighbouring Catalina Island and the Pacific Ocean.

Photography: Dennis Anderson

Kotze House

Hugo Hamity Architects

The Kotze House is located in an old, traditional suburb, on a tennis court subdivision for a couple who runs a business from the adjacent cottage on the property. The tennis court is on a lower level than the street so access to the house is on the first floor through a split-level.

Externally, the garden is flanked by a line of trees on the perimeter that marks the edge of the lap pool. Different landscape textures recall the original dimensions of the tennis court and the old ground while allowing the old ground to breathe after decades of being covered over with concrete.

White on the walls, and natural concrete flooring allow for a continuous source of inspiration for change enhancing natural and neutral material and colours.

Photography: Karin Brady

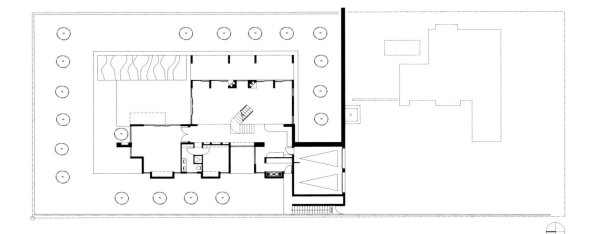

Halum Residence

Designed for a family with children, this house has outdoor living spaces and wraps around a curvilinear pool.

Celebrating the prevalent desert climate, an outdoor living room with a massive fireplace and roof with cedar ceiling overhang, provide an escape few can resist.

The multi-level pool deck area offers a swim-up bar and is surrounded by the sights and peaceful sounds of waterfalls. The meandering edge of the reflecting pool and an engraved curving pattern on the walkway give the residents and guests a revealing visual experience every step of the way leading to the entry door.

The front gate area of the house was designed to create a ceremonial welcoming environment for guests. From the front gate to the back door and everywhere in between, natural stone, steel, wood, glass and water are predominant in the house's design.

Photography: Nicola Pira

Patel Architecture/Narendra Patel, AIA

Quincho II

This 'quincho' or 'eating place' was constructed as an addition to an existing house. The feel of this structure is native, yet primitive. The extension is built of recycled wood.

This small space has an uncluttered feel to it. The traditional table of a quincho is the focal point and the bench seating and table is fixed using near-invisible fixtures. The benches are covered with cowhide.

The flooring is of rustic field fencing embracing primitive technology with the romanticism of native folklore.

Photography: Gustavo Frittegotto

Rafael Iglesia Arquitectos

Murad Ismail House

MADIWELA, KOTTE, SRI LANKA

MICD Associates

The site was originally a stone excavation site for more than 50 years. It was on a higher level than the road and sloped upward ending in a ridge with a large Jak* tree.

Designed in two rectilinear blocks along boundaries perpendicular to the road, the house was connected with a lightweight 'bridge' structure set out carefully on site in order to save two great trees. The outdoor spaces consist of an arc-shaped stairway leading from the lower level of the garden to a paved courtyard. Large garden benches provide outdoor seating and a view over the garden.

Enormous trees that were conserved on the site and tropical shrubs like frangipani and hibiscus provide shade and a sense of serene tranquillity.

*Bot. Artocarpus hetrophyllus – belongs to the Moracae family, an evergreen tree that grows to over 18 metres. Prized for its fruit and its wood, the trees have large, densely foliated branches that provide a high degree of shade.

Photography: Chamika De Alwis

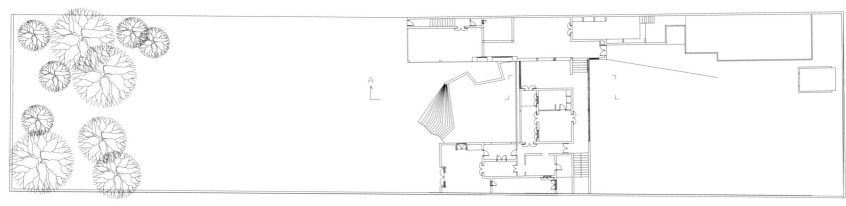

Private Penthouse

Studio Gaia

This penthouse located on the 71st floor of a tall building is a virtual oasis in the midst of bustling New York City. The owner required a place to dream in peace, for solitude and creative thought; being so high above the busy city, the outdoor spaces are relatively quiet and calm.

The penthouse is a two-storey, spacious abode. The outdoor space consists of a large terrace that opens out from the living room. Despite the elevation of this terrace, an area of lush turf provides a sense of being on ground level. Ample seating provides facilities for both entertaining and relaxing. Illuminated trees provide a magical incandescence at night and the surrounding buildings serve as the only reminder that this terrace is indeed in the heart of busy, metropolitan New York City.

Photography: Moon Lee

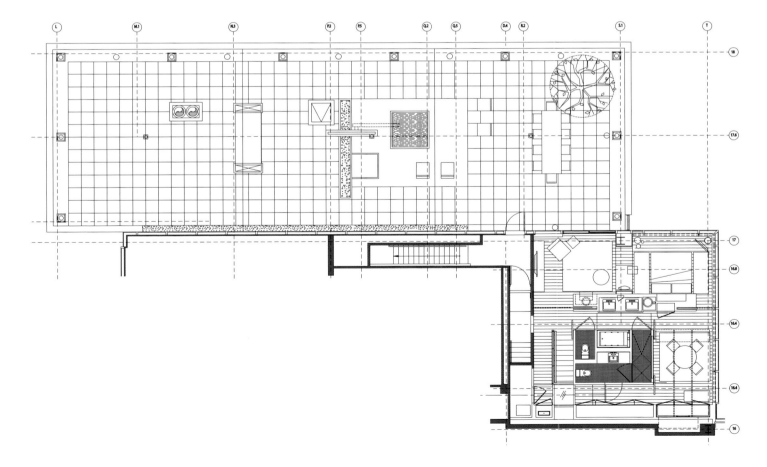

House AVI Michael

Hugo Hamity Architects

For many years in Johannesburg, traditional old suburbs have been subdivided into smaller portions of land with the aim to grow extended families or 'densification'. This house is a new residence on a narrow and irregular subdivision with no building line restrictions.

Exterior and interior architecture are fused together by the visual and spatial experience. At first glance the house appears to open and reveal all its different components – the open garden and the main bedroom space. A visual link allows for the connection between the two prominent volumes of the public and private areas while retaining a north western orientated open garden.

Other pockets such as open courtyards project a feeling of unrestricted living. The use of white symbolises an open canvas where colour and texture is introduced by lifestyle.

Photography: Karin Brady

Sudbury Residence

SUDBURY, MASSACHUSETTS ON WILLIS POND, USA

Hammer Architects

An addition and renovation to a contemporary home in Sudbury added a new dining room, guest suite, garage, home office and an indoor swimming pool with adjacent changing and exercise rooms.

Exposed timber framing, wood ceilings and custom mahogany doors enclose the new lap pool that leads directly outside to a courtyard featuring Vermont bluestone pavers, and granite, and landscaped with native wetland shrubs and plants. Lighting is integrated into the granite kerbing, which defines the edge of the paved courtyard and delineates the circulation, cooking and entertainment areas. Paths from the courtyard lead to the pond where canoes are docked.

The open roof deck above the pool structure is accessed from the living room and guest suite and provides an overlook of the adjacent pond. The addition and existing building form a vehicular courtyard in the front of the house that access the four garages. The courtyard is planted with flowering vines and lilies.

Photography: Grieg Cranna

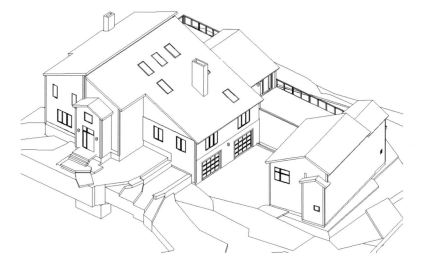

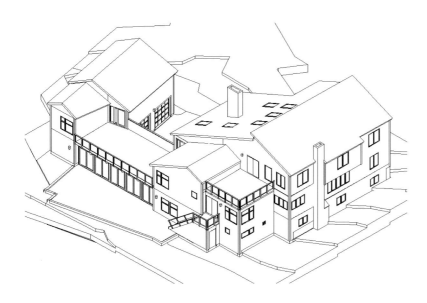

G House

Datumzero Design Office

The G House is located in the borough of Fort Lee, three miles west of New York City, across the Hudson river. Given the zoning constraints in the area, most residences have a 7.5 metre set back on the rear yards. These yards become an open space with a lack of definition.

The patio in the G House is an interesting mix of programs that define very specific uses for small spaces. The various uses range from a secluded jacuzzi, seating areas and cooking bar, to a sunbathing niche. The entire patio is an extension of the dining room and open kitchen. Stepping out of the interior, a plant-filled wood deck leads to a random stone patio floor. The patio is defined by built-in wood benches and planters that provide privacy to the jacuzzi area.

Most surfaces in the patio area consist of materials adaptable to summer and winter changes such as stone, wood decking, crushed stone and mulch. while wood planters of various sizes allow for seasonal planting.

Soft lighting at night provides a cosy environment for family gatherings and for a very large part of the summer, indoor activities such as cooking, dining and breakfast take place out on the patio.

Photography: Frank Schwere Photography

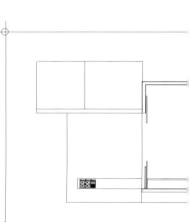

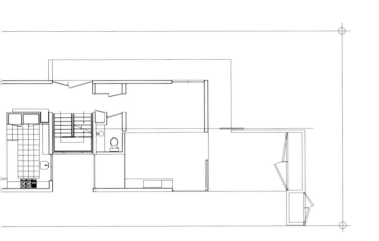

Lambrakis House

Hugo Hamity Architects

This house is situated on a mountain slope and overlooks Johannesburg on the western horizon. The design is an orthogonal grid around a central circular staircase. The staircase determines the geometries of the external covered spaces such as the entrance portico, private courtyards and the double-volume covered patio.

The double-volume covered patio is positioned to take advantage of the setting sun in the west and also to keep rainwater off the external couches, tables and chairs. The interior bar opens onto this patio.

A basement occupies a gap between the pool and the natural slope of the terrain. Large windows in the basement entertainment area overlook the infinite pool providing a sense of unity between indoors and outdoors.

Photography: Karin Brady

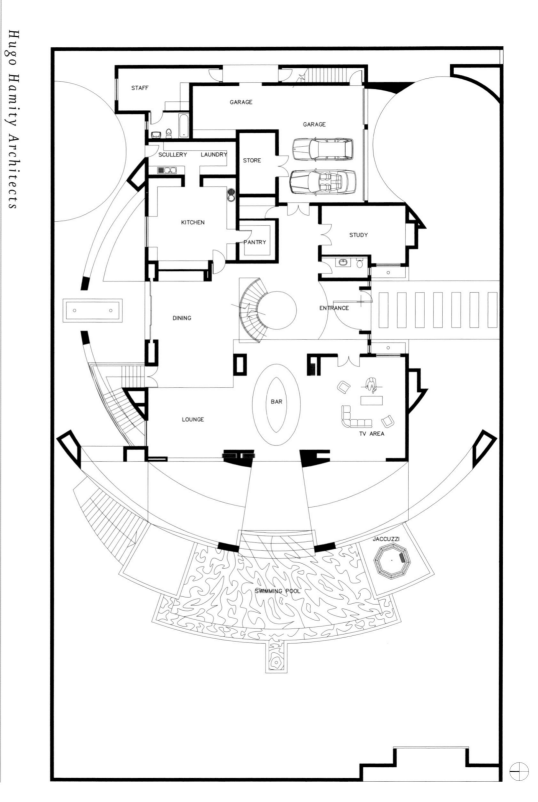

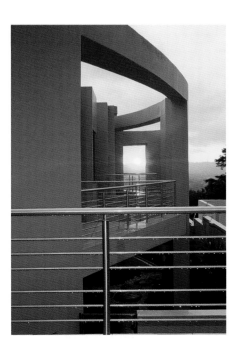

Yautepec Residence

Pascal Arquitectos

This house is sited on a piece of land that had been reclaimed from an acre of cornfields. An hour-and-a-half away from Mexico City, the climatic conditions here are extreme; with hot, dry winters and warm, rainy summers.

The building is composed of two, separate building wings. Designed with specific consideration for the landscape and the view towards the Tepozteco mountains, shady areas have been created using pergolas and a wide variety of plants and trees.

The outdoor spaces act as an extension of the enclosed spaces, encouraging occupants to move around the dwelling. A broad bower, covered with vines, provides protection against light and heat for both buildings. The landscape surrounding the buildings was a conditioning factor for the design of the garden, with the characteristic climate of the site taken into account. More than a hundred different species of orchids, as well as zapote, banana, tamarind, papaya and guava trees constitute the great variety of vegetation. Many other design elements make up the integral form of the outdoor spaces. These include sequence, spontaneity and organic forms, that ensure the garden does not appear prefabricated, but blends effortlessly with nature.

Photography: Alberto Moreno

Casa en Fisherton

Rafael Iglesia Arquitectos

This house located on a site surrounded by nature is rather spare in comparison to its verdant surroundings.

It appears to be in an inner street that culminates in a Roman-style patio. The entry appears almost ceremonial and has its own autonomous character despite it being the link between the inside and outside.

Outdoor living spaces consist of an open yard on one side, and an uncluttered patio with paved stones alongside the entry. The design scheme is minimalist and multi-functional.

Photography: Gustavo Frittegotto

Tel Barauch Residence

Arcod Architects

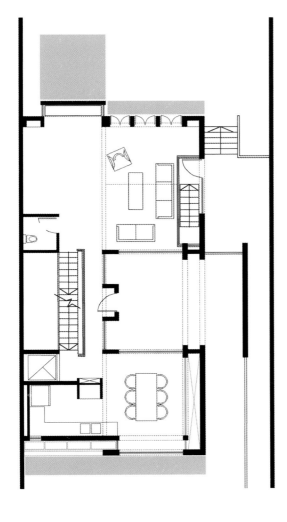

This three-storey residence is located in a crowded, Tel Aviv neighbourhood. Despite its location, the outdoor spaces exude serenity and calm behind walls that shut out the noise of the city.

The house has been built around a courtyard and stairwell and consists of two wings. Horizontal passageways that close outward and turn inward to face the courtyard connect the two wings.

Outdoor seating provides a welcoming area for alfresco meals and entertaining. With ornamental plants and trees with dense foliage, the garden is a quiet place that is well protected from the bustle of the urban life outside the walls.

Photography: Amit Geron

Achio House

SANTA ANA, SAN JOSE, COSTA RICA

Datumzero Design Office

Contextually, this home was designed around three distinct areas: the pool, the interior and the green areas. Each area is connected by an oval-shaped space with a stained concrete finish.

All yards connect through the large door systems with openings up to five metres. These openings dissolve the boundaries between the interior and exterior completely. Both dining and living rooms become thresholds and function as shelter from the sun for the yards.

The interior yard offers views to the other yards through the dining and living room. The green yard is larger and is planted with trees, foliage and grass. The pool yard generates energy and activity with its blue body of water, the cabana and close access to the kitchen, making it a perfect place for leisure and entertaining.

Photography: Frank Schwere Photography

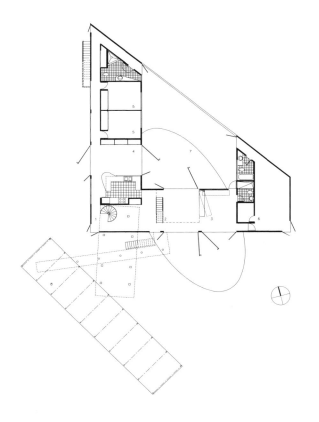

Rogers Residence

San Luis Obispo, California, USA

Jeffrey Gordon Smith Landscape Architecture

This residence is located on a high-profile downtown street. A low architectural wall with a traditional-style gate results in an outdoor space that is pleasing and restful. A large water feature in the centre of the garden adds to the ambience. The garden has a Mediterranean feel containing several plants with rough-textures.

The home's limited interior drove the need for the exterior landscape to include as much entertainment and escape spaces as possible. The owners' personal training business, is located in the backyard garden and design amenities include an outdoor kitchen, fireplace, shower, plunge pool, pergola, lounge areas, fresh water features and a hookah* room.

The backyard is an oasis-like escape with water features influencing each space. A strong axis projects through the plunge pool that is terminated by a large urn in the back of the garden and an outdoor shower against the house. The gym opens out onto the pool and is connected to the space by architectural columns and a pergola that leads down to the lower terrace. A warm fireplace is the focal point of this room, which is opposed by a one-metre overflow from the pool.

*An Asian pipe for smoking tobacco or marijuana, consisting of a flexible tube with a mouthpiece attached to a container of water through which smoke is drawn and cooled. Also called hubble-bubble or narghile.

Photography: Elliot Johnson

Theisen House

BRADENTON, FLORIDA, USA

Guy Peterson/Office for Architecture, Inc.

This large 900-square-metre house is located on a long, thin linear site with the narrow end overlooking a large bay to a barrier island on the Gulf of Mexico. In manipulating the scale of this house by 'eroding' the geometric forms, the house separates itself into smaller forms. Between these forms, a variety of courtyard spaces are created.

The Entry Water Courtyard threads through the short axis of the house and serves as a transitional space. With a shallow pool of water and a continuous waterfall, it adds a soothing sound.

The Pool Courtyard is a private space with the main house entertainment room on one side. It opens out into the guesthouse living room on the other side.

The private, large Gazing Ball Courtyard is located to the rear of the guesthouse and celebrates a large live oak tree. A 3.6-metre grid is established between this tree and another further to the south. Marking this grid, are 37 silver gazing balls all located 93 centimetres above grade. These reflect the house and natural environment. Centred in the courtyard is a small piazza for relaxation. The upper terrace of the guesthouse overlooks this garden courtyard.

Photography: Steven Brooke Studios

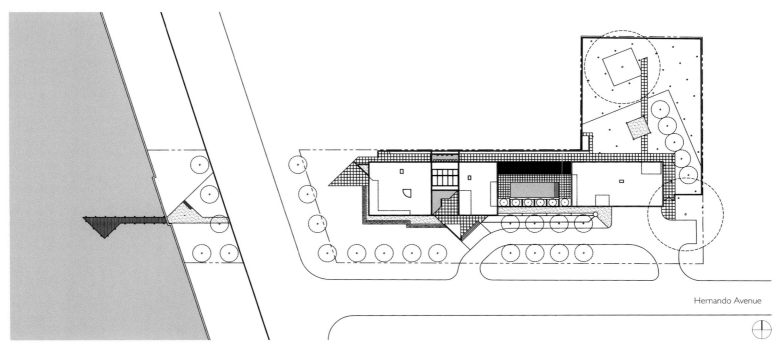

Hernando Avenue

Aarthun Residence

BIGHORN CANYONS, PALM DESERT, CALIFORNIA, USA

Patel Architecture/Narendra Patel, AIA

Designed as a 'living sculpture' this home encompasses over 557 square metres of living area offering a dramatic and unique juxtaposition of contrasting architectural elements.

This desert home turns a weather-toughened stone-clad face to the street and provides a sheltered forecourt. A large steel gate opens to the entry courtyard. Sliding glass doors disappear mysteriously into the walls, dissolving the boundary between indoors and out.

Surrounded by a large deck and entertainment area, the patio offers breathtaking, panoramic views of the valley while the pool captures the imagination with an outcrop of semi-submerged boulders. Appearing to cascade into the pool, these boulders blend with the surrounding desert. The outdoor living area includes the outdoor living room with fireplace, outdoor kitchen, and large entertainment area around the pool.

Photography: Nicola Pira

Felix Residence

Jeffrey Gordon Smith Landscape Architecture

A small front landscape played an important role in transforming the kerbside appeal of this large residence and integrated the kitchen and dining room. The property is a flag lot with a shared driveway easement that is dominated by the garages of both this house and that of the neighbours.

A dramatic new entry focal point was created with a steel and sandblasted glass screen designed to provide interest and privacy. The carport is made from scored concrete that echoes the grid pattern of the privacy screen.

The original entry was moved outside by choreographing the carport to open into an entry courtyard via a pivot gate. Visitors to the area are attracted to a water wall that offers a close and tactile experience. The larger expanse of water is overlooked from the dining room. The water wall appears to flow down into the reflecting pool before spilling into a copper slit on the deck. The ipe wood deck is enclosed and sheltered from the coastal winds of nearby Shell Beach. It is enhanced by the fire-pit filled with recycled glass that heats the entertainment space at night.

The interior planter incorporates an impressive floral arrangement that includes many exotic plant species. The screen not only provides privacy for this interior garden but also a backdrop to what could be an undesirable view and allows morning eastern light to enter the garden. At night, the screen's dramatic lighting changes the mood with colours changing from soft yellow tones to vivid pinks, reds and blues.

Photography: Darren Marsan

Villa HJ

Architectenbureau Paul de Ruiter B.V.

Villa HJ was built with two objectives in mind: to have a practical and private dwelling and to maximise the views of the surrounding nature. With this in mind, the villa is built around a glass patio. Despite this patio giving the house a private feel it also has a key role. It contains the entrance and organises the route through the villa.

The walls surrounding the patio are made of glass and bring light deep into the structure. The walls at the neighbour's side are more closed heightening the sense of security, privacy and calm. The fully glazed south side wall takes advantage of the fact that there are no neighbours and has a spectacular view over the surrounding marshland.

Photography: Alessio Guarino, Rien van Rijthoven

Frank Residence

Positioned to enjoy the tranquil lake views and surrounding mountains, this home is organised as a cluster of interconnected parts. Overlapping fragments evoke images of a seaside village with courtyards and terraces.

Designed for outdoor living, all rooms in the house open onto private patios and pool terraces, providing wondrous places to read, dine, sun or enjoy cocktails and conversation.

Key elements encourage the harmonious blending of indoor/outdoor spaces. The sweeping, copper-covered curved roof lifts open and creates an illusion of space literally exploding open to bring the outdoors in. The atrium courtyard is located deep within the plan and brings in natural light and cross-ventilation.

Light reflecting off the calm surface and the play and movement of the lake induces a deep sense of tranquillity while the infinity-edged pool beside the lake is almost other-worldly. Surrounded by spectacular views, the experience of being in one's own heaven is simply sublime.

Photography: Nicola Pira

Patel Architecture/Narendra Patel, AIA

Christian Residence

SAN LUIS OBISPO, CALIFORNIA, USA

Jeffrey Gordon Smith, Landscape Architecture

This ranch-style home needed an update that would take advantage of the expansive views of Cerro San Luis and the Edna Valley and provide an indoor-outdoor lifestyle. The garden update was also to match the architecture and the clients' love of early, modern furnishings.

Retro 1950s circular shapes dominate the landscape creating a fun, modern, outdoor mood. Rounded concrete entry steps lead to the first circular entry threshold and are echoed in the door thresholds and the corners of the home. The front main patio and the back patio also incorporate the circle theme in their amoeba-like shaping. In both patios, circle planter voids are cut in the concrete and circular glass pieces add interest. Beacon-like light changes at night. A pre-cast concrete seat wall with circular blue glass inlay mimics the front patio shape and provides a viewing seat to enjoy the scenery.

Photography: Elliot Johnson

Mermaid Beach House

Rust Architecture Design

The owners of this house, a busy, professional couple with two children, required a house that made the best use of the beachside lifestyle. The architects created a new dimension for Queensland living based on a 'pavilion style' that incorporated efficient space planning and appropriate site layout and orientation.

'The outdoor room is the new Queensland veranda' was the belief of the architects, and this made a major contribution to the entire design. Simple, classic forms were applied to achieve a sense of tropical living and a seamless blend of inside and out. Roof overhangs, natural cross-flow ventilation and open-plan living areas enhanced this easy transition from indoors to outdoors.

A courtyard with seating allows the family to entertain with ease as it adjoins the kitchen. Even the garage is a multi-purpose space that can be screened off with sliding screens or opened to extend the outdoor living spaces. Well-proportioned spaces, natural light, simple materials and finishes and great connection to the outdoors capture the spirit of Australian coastal living.

Photography: Millar Photography

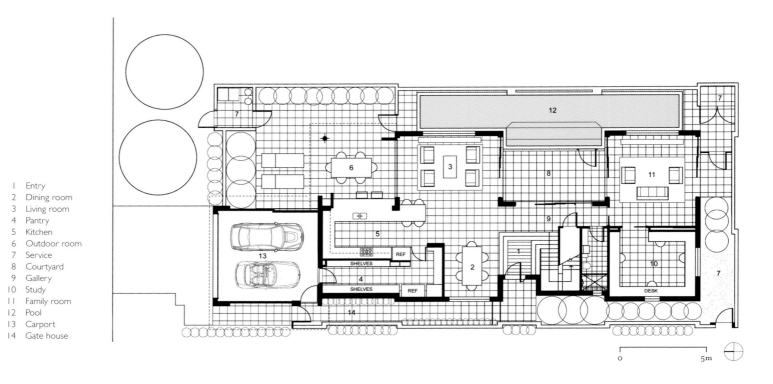

1 Entry
2 Dining room
3 Living room
4 Pantry
5 Kitchen
6 Outdoor room
7 Service
8 Courtyard
9 Gallery
10 Study
11 Family room
12 Pool
13 Carport
14 Gate house

Jensen Residence

SAN LUIS OBISPO, CALIFORNIA, USA

Jeffrey Gordon Smith Landscape Architecture

To visually enlarge this backyard garden, the courtyard was designed on a grid turned at a 45-degree angle. The grid is defined by a series of redwood squares filled with loose Mexican pebbles with pavers laid out on the grid as the garden pathway. Water sheets flow down passive concrete water columns that vary in height and diameter and are placed in a gravel basin where a sump re-circulates the water.

At the far end of the garden, the focal point is a basalt column that serves as a point of reflection and a birdbath. *Pittosporum tenuifolium* (silver sheen) creates a hedge that defines the outside edge of the garden room playing off the various foliage textures to reinforce the grid of the garden. This east-facing courtyard receives the glorious morning sun and becomes a Zen escape for a peaceful, reflective breakfast.

Photography: Elliot Johnson

House in Sakakida

Satoshi Okada architects

Sakakida, in the northern district of Kyoto, is a grid formation where the ancient urban fabric still exists. Once known for its grand residences owned by rich merchants, today it has been broken into tiny housing lots due to the high inheritance taxation.

The house is a three-storey vertical and a two-storey horizontal volume in which a garden and terrace are contained. Interior spaces can be opened totally to the exterior terrace and balcony that are on a platform at the first level.

The terrace is heated by sunlight. When the living quarter is opened, cool air at the ground-level garden is pulled up into it. This ancient system known as machiya* is based on ingenious Japanese vernacular architecture, which requires two tiny gardens. One is easily warmed, the other is not, and they function as a wind generator that passes through interior space.

*Machiya are traditional wooded townhouses found throughout Japan and typified in the historical capital of Kyoto. The etymology of the word machiya reveals its two parts: machi – meaning 'town' and ya – meaning 'house'.

Photography: courtesy Satoshi Okada architects

Casa de las Estrellas

House + House Architects/Cathi House

Abounding with gardens and light, this 186-square-metre home's exterior spaces appear ethereal. The living spaces open onto a plant-filled courtyard. An arc of burnished concrete columns open the master bedroom to a private garden and the master bath wraps around an ancient, pomegranate tree. Bedrooms above share a covered terrace overlooking the courtyard. The oak entry door opens to a sinuous stairway and frosted stars sparkle against a tall, blue wall. Floor-to-ceiling windows open each room to the light, linking inside to out.

Luscious colours of mango, cobalt and grey-green are lime washes toned with natural minerals. River rocks in red and ochre, set against a charcoal background, swirl on the courtyard floor while slate is tightly fitted into random patterns inside. Burgundy concrete accents adorn stairs and wrap the columns. Rusted, perforated-steel sconces, skylights and railings cast shadows and light patterns into unexpected places. Materials and construction techniques are traditional, yet the forms are modern and in total alignment with the sun, wind and views.

Photography: Steven House

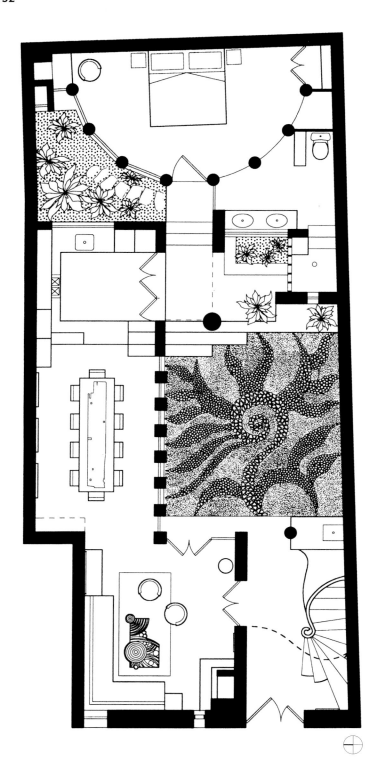

Hamity Parkin House

Hugo Hamity Architects

This 1930s house was renovated to update it to contemporary standards while preserving its character. Situated on an elevated contour, both vehicular and pedestrian access is through an existing embankment that allows ground and rain water to flow freely along its slope.

Sandstone cladding on existing walls makes for easy maintenance of the street-facing walls. On the other side, it becomes a focal point from which springs the living area across a tiered courtyard that makes use of the embankment's slope.

The tiered courtyard defines the arrival and living areas while keeping on the original slope. A new pergola that conceptually forms the entrance stoep* to the original house adds to the heritage value. Local, natural materials, such as the wall cladding and timber for external elements and walking areas, achieve a sustainable architectural environment.

*stoep - porch, verandah, like American stoop but pronounced with a shorter vowel

Photography: Karin Brady

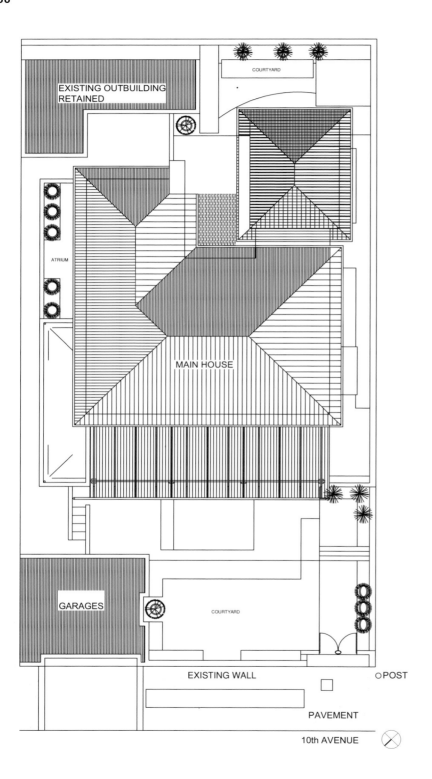

EXISTING OUTBUILDING RETAINED

COURTYARD

ATRIUM

MAIN HOUSE

GARAGES

COURTYARD

EXISTING WALL

POST

PAVEMENT

10th AVENUE

Petrolivano

Aiolou Architects

A couple of stone walls was all that remained of the original house on this plot of land in southern Greece. Amazingly, the entrance with carved stone arch and keystones adorned with mysterious relief-sculpted animals, had survived through time. The site dates back to the 15th century and the original phase of the house and part of the ruins were of Byzantine origin dating back to the 17th century. Stunning views both towards the Mediterranean and up to the Taygetos mountains, which overlook the village from the east, were an added bonus.

In Greece, outdoor living is possible for around eight months of the year and the verandas and courtyards were built to accommodate this lifestyle. Eating, relaxing and entertaining, even the occasional afternoon nap, are possible on the sheltered outdoor spaces. These additional outdoor living spaces opened up the house to the magnificent views up the gorge and down to the sea.

Apart from the stone of the original building, additional stone came from a local quarry to match the original. The terraces are laid in a type of slate known locally as 'Albanian'. Recycled bricks and chiselled sandstone make up the steps and borders and local mud was mixed into the pointing and the cement tops of the stone benches to blend with the original colours. Cypress tree trunks support a bamboo pergola.

Photography: Nikos Xanthopoulos

Landscape Architect Studio

Marcelo Novaes Paisagismo

This design provides a showcase for the owner's exotic orchids and also an opportunity to create a tranquil retreat and seek artistic inspiration.

Natural materials formed the scheme of the design incorporating wood, rock and water to transform the exterior spaces into calm and restful areas with a Zen feel. The garden houses the owner's plants and the wooden pergola functions as a greenhouse and laboratory for his research and experiments. Constructed of seasoned wood coated in protective varnish, it is an ideal place to work in peaceful surrounds.

A pathway of rock, lined on either side with bottle palms meanders across the greenhouses and leads to the studio and orchid arbour. A large palm tree stands in the centre of the greenhouses. The greenhouses and inner courtyard paved in flagstones of Goia rock, are visible from the studio.

Water is a central theme in the design scheme. To one side of the pergola lies a mirror-like, pebble-lined pond, while the relaxing sounds of water emanate from a sculpture pond on the other side.

Photography: Ricardo Rodrigues Breda

Casa Santa Fe

Daniel Perez-Gil Arquitectos

Located on a sloping site, this house is built on three levels with pedestrian and vehicular access via the basement. Pedestrian access from the street is through a curved wall from which a marble stairway leads. A waterfall runs parallel and is crowned by a crystal dome that leads to the main lobby.

The exterior living spaces comprise a dining area and bar that lead to the garden off the living room. Located at the rear of the property, these areas maximise the utilisation of the ample garden spaces.

With a distinct avant-garde feel to the design, use of materials such as wood, crystal and clever lighting heighten the style and elegance of these spaces.

Photography: Hector Armando Herrera

Parkside Residence

Studio 9 Architects

An addition to this turn-of-the-20th century villa was designed to reflect the Australian indoor/outdoor lifestyle. The contemporary design scheme aimed to complement but not replicate the original house. Because the older part of the house offered little opportunity for flexibility of indoor/outdoor lifestyle, the new addition aimed to fill that void.

The limited allotment size demanded that the rear portion of the driveway doubles as an outdoor meals area while the balance of the space is dedicated to outdoor activities. The outdoor rooms are divided into two distinct but linked zones.

Each space has been designed to offer maximum functionality both internally and externally and accommodate a variety of family activities while expressing a contemporary Australian lifestyle.

Photography: Sarah Long Photography

Ateliers de Santa Catarina

This spare, minimalist house is located on a site with an olive grove to the east and a view of the San Francisco hills to the south. After successive studies, a number of conditioning factors relevant to the programme – sunlight and the internal/external visual relationships – changed the typology. This created a wide range of archetypal spaces which recall the traditions of the region. The residence is set on a raised rectangular platform where the various interior spaces define and complement the outdoor areas.

The patio set between walls reflects the southern light entering the living room off its white wall to the north. A greenhouse located at the southwest end completes the arrangement.

Photography: Pedro Rogado, Catarina Almada Negreiros

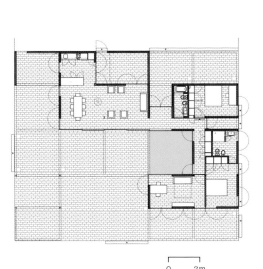

0   3m

Webster Residence

VENICE, CALIFORNIA, USA

Steven Ehrlich Architects

This residence utilises the oasis of an interior courtyard as an antidote to the urban context. Just a half block from the beach, the rectangular lot fronts a walk street, one of only a handful of streets closed to traffic in Venice. The design provides a cohesive plan that is pulled apart to leave an internal tranquil courtyard at its centre.

The building consists of two volumes at each end of a lot, linked by a service spine on the east and a central courtyard complete with a reflecting pool. Framed steel I-beams frame roll-up glass doors on the two façades that face the courtyard and the front façade that links the walk-street. This open axis provides an unparalleled level of clear space. The amphitheatre-like steps that rise from the courtyard further enhance this procession of space. The raised platform not only provides an additional vantage point to enjoy the exterior but it also moderates the site's 1.5 metre rise in grade from front to back.

The courtyard spaces moderate the warm summer temperatures and provide a comfortable microclimate through lush plantings and running water. It successfully exploits the benign climate of southern California to maximise indoor/outdoor living. Several upper level terraces and a large roof deck allow private and public venues to enjoy the views of the Pacific.

Photography: Benny Chan

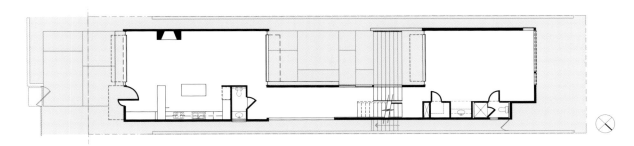

Nautilus

The approach to this house is through metal gates that lead to the front courtyard. The sculptural form, natural materials, soft desert colours and curving walls complement the overall design scheme.

The outdoor living areas are extensions of the indoor living spaces. The sweeping curved shape of the pool is in harmony with the shape of the roof. The hovering, vaulted ceiling with its concealed support intensifies the sense of drama and creates the illusion of a floating cover to this indoor/outdoor visual living experience.

The ceiling itself is tongue-and-groove wood, set in a directional manner that enhances visual effect by leading the eye from the external space, through to the indoors and back outdoors again. The wood ceiling is punctured with a myriad of small, halogen lights creating the effect of a star-studded sky.

Photography: Arthur Coleman

Patel Architecture/Narendra Patel, AIA

House in C.U.B.A.

Maletti Zanel Maletti Maletti Arquitectos

The undulating terrain of this site inspired the house and in turn, created special and interesting spaces within it while solving functional needs.

The principal access is on the first floor. The ground floor contains the bedrooms. These areas follow the natural slope of the land. Non-orthogonal architectural geometry ensures that the trees and surrounding vegetation are preserved and gives way to three courtyards.

The Access Courtyard contains the entrance and links the neighbours. On the other side lays the Stair Courtyard, a quiet, calm place with views throughout the house. The Major Courtyard is a dynamic and active area and is shielded from the street. It contains the pool, the barbeque and the annexe containing the bedrooms. The courtyards are planted with native Palo Borracho (*chorisia insignis*) trees known for their inverted leaves. This characteristic permits the sun to stream into the house in winter and protects it in summer. Large glass windows permit a close bonding with the courtyards.

Photography: Carlos Olmos

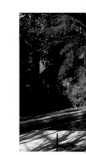

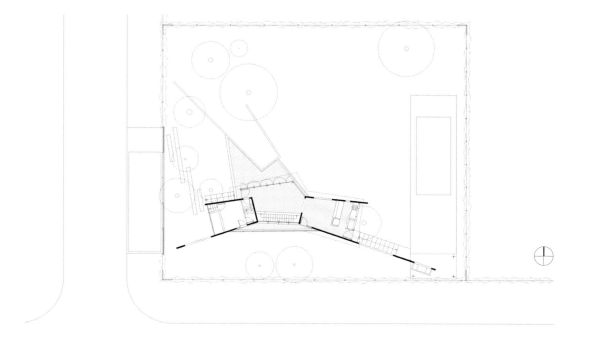

The Divide House

This home sits atop the Cordillera Rocky mountains in central Colorado, in a development that is inspired by the regions of southern and central Europe. Essentially based on the rural building designs of Belgium, the Catalonian region of Spain and the southern and central provinces of France, the structure has repetitive forms in the French country-style.

The outdoor living spaces comprise a small courtyard paved in an irregular paving pattern, complete with seating arrangements. Informal and relaxed, it is an area to enjoy the spectacular views and the invigorating air of this high-altitude region of Colorado.

The garden has a rustic, casual feel with an affinity to the spectacular nature that surrounds this site.

Photography: David O. Marlow

Paddle Creek Design/Thom Oppelt, Architect

Diorama

Two massive and planar volumes loosely divide this open plan space into kitchen, living and dining areas. These new areas open onto a small, decked courtyard. The internal floor is diamond-ground concrete, contrasting with the pine decking of the courtyard.

White-painted timber-glazed doors link the internal and external spaces. Views through the spaces to the small courtyard are carefully controlled to provide only glimpses and allow partial comprehension. This visual choreography creates an impression of a larger, more complex space.

The courtyard is treated as an external room and this is reinforced by the equivalent sizing of the internal spaces. The interior concrete floor finish has perhaps greater external connotations than the timber that lines the courtyard at the same level as the interior.

Photography: William Tozer Architecture & Design

William Tozer Architecture & Design

Residence in Campinas

Marcelo Novaes Paisagismo

The exterior spaces of this residence project the feel of a true oasis. Despite being a relatively small area, the garden and surroundings are full of surprising diversity. While complementing the architecture of the house on the site, a wealth of plants, trees, water and nature merge together in a very pleasing fusion. Spread on several levels, the design of the garden aesthetically combines exotic plants, natural elements like rock, stone and water.

The visitor is greeted by a grouping of fox-tail palms upon entering the garden. A profusion of bromeliads and bottle plants grace the irregular, rough-hewn rock pathways. A pentagon-shaped gazebo sheltered by wooden beams sits on an elevated level. Serving as an observation point to enjoy the surrounding beauty and soothe the spirit, it also has comfortable seating. From the gazebo, rough rock-hewn steps lead in an irregular pattern to a pond filled with red and gold ornamental carp. Water cascading from the side of the pond provides soothing sounds and promotes a feeling of total relaxation.

Interspersed between the rocks, both on the grass and the side of the pond, are many tropical plant species such as bromeliads and asparagus ferns, while papyrus reeds abound on the edge of the pond. Much care and consideration have been given to little details such as the colour schemes of the plants – a thicket of bright crimson-hued bromeliads provides stark contrast to the pale-coloured gravel and dark glossy-green philodendrons combine with brightly coloured crotons.

Photography: Gustavo Olmas

Solar Deck

Driendl* Architects

The 14th district of Vienna is a typical, suburban village district. Its residents enjoy a high living standard in private houses that are mostly situated on small, tight sites. This site was also rather small and situated in a densely populated area.

Despite these constraints Solar Deck projects a feeling of complete weightlessness. The bedrooms and other living areas are all located on the ground floor while the kitchen and living room are located on the upper floor. A self-supporting steel structure, this floor is open and spacious and because of the absence of columns projects a feeling of total fluidity.

A number of outdoor spaces emerge, as a part of this floor is widened with co-relating terraces on the east, south and west sides. The result is the effect of the living room appearing to increase over the terraces pushing neighbouring structures into the distance.

In keeping with the concept of maximising sunlight, large areas of glazing and a transparent strip along the north side of the roof floods the area with light and fulfil the architect's aim of bringing "daylight into the smallest corner".

Photography: Lew Rodin

Overmyer Residence

Perched on a west-facing hillside, north of San Francisco, with spectacular views to Mount Tamalpias, this new home gently embraces its site.

Comprised of two intersecting wings, the connecting tower's inverted butterfly roof frames the mountain peak. To take advantage of the limited flat area of the site, the L-shaped home is pushed to the slope to wrap around a level, garden courtyard.

This courtyard is the primary outdoor space for relaxation, play and entertaining. Sunlight pours into the terraced gardens laced with sculpted walkways, to the spa, the rear entry and the children's play area. A wide ribbon of water spills from the wall into a cool fountain outside the dining room window, sending ripples of sound and reflections of light. Thickened red stucco walls frame doorways, marking portals between the home and the lush courtyard.

Photography: David Duncan Livingston

House + House Architects/Cathi House

Casa Mar Azul

Besonias Almeida Kruk Arquitectos

Mar Azul or 'Blue Sea' is a town on the coast of Buenos Aires, 12 kilometres from the seaside resort of Villa Gesell. It is characterised by large expanses of virgin dune beach on the one side and lush, coniferous forest on the other. The owners of this house required a small, unobtrusive house to be used in the summertime. The house had to be low-maintenance and most importantly, blend with the landscape as much as possible.

Set in a grove of 43 pine trees, the structure is devoid of concrete. In total harmony with the verdant forest, it has one fully glazed side. The outdoor living spaces consist of an ample wooden deck that seems to be the main focus. Wooden accents throughout predominate and even the furniture is of Canadian pine reconstituted from packing crates that contained engine spare parts.

Photography: Maria Victoria Besonias,
Guillermo de Almeida

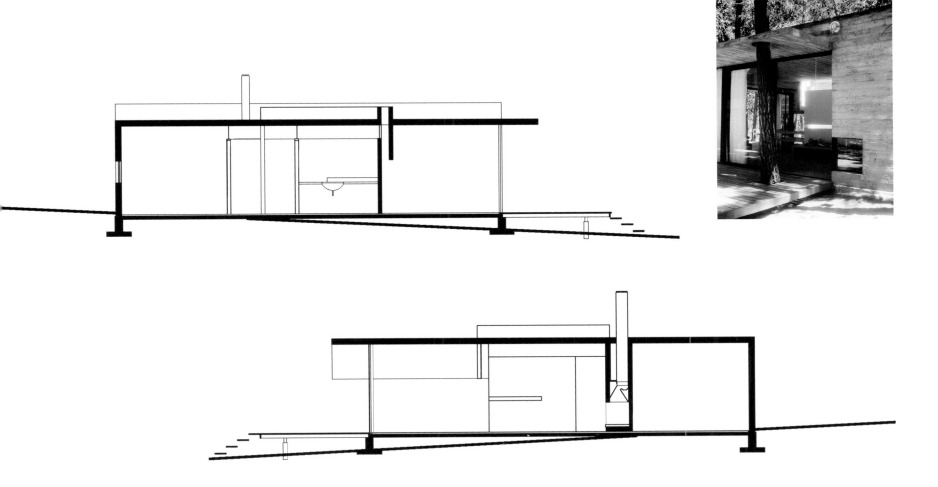

Casa Breva del Lago

Paddle Creek Design/Vesta Development

Tuscan-style Casa Breva del Lago in western United States at Lake Las Vegas Resort, is built around a 130-hectare, three-kilometre-long, manmade lake.

Two separate courtyards serve distinct purposes for this 550-square-metre home. One helps define the entry while the other creates a separate, more private, living and dining experience.

The entry courtyard has a brick-paved driveway and leads visitors past the cascading waterfalls of the negative edge pool, to the carport. A stone wall and iron gate lead to the open air courtyard entry with distinctive Italian styling, from the stone tile pavers to the stone-and-stucco exterior. Two wrought-iron balconies, that overlook the courtyard and exposed heavy timber detailing complete the look of timeless warmth.

Entry from the garage leads to the other south-facing courtyard and rose garden. It serves as a serene space for outdoor living and dining. A covered sitting area with stone tile pavers and an outdoor kitchen complements this space. Two pocket windows make this rear courtyard accessible from indoors and when these pocket walls disappear, big open spaces are created for entertaining.

Photography: VHT

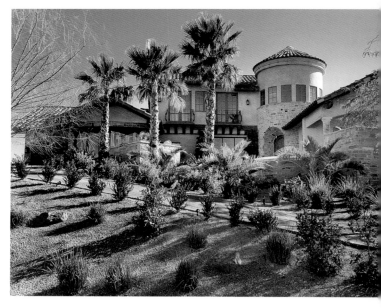

Casa de las Buenas Almas

CABO PULMO, BAJA CALIFORNIA, MEXICO

House + House Architects/Cathi House

In a small fishing village on the sea of Cortes in Baja, Mexico, this home is a compound of three buildings woven among trees and cactus, which forms a central courtyard. Framing the courtyard is the main building, comprised of a master suite that sits above the living area; a separate *casita** for guests, which adds a beautiful feature in the vistas of the compound and a garage wall composed of scattered glass blocks.

Palapa**-covered terraces and gardens seamlessly connect the inside with the outside. Outdoor dining and wide, built-in benches offer perfect areas for relaxation. A soft, purple haze in the mountain backdrop, with bold outcroppings of salmon-coloured rock, provides the inspiration for the colours of this home. Broad windows and multiple terraces capture the breezes and views. Ancient hacienda doors give this contemporary home a touch of the old world.

The remote location comes without the clutter of power lines. Electricity is gathered from the sun and stored to provide power for lighting and all the comforts of home.

*Casita – chalet or guesthouse
**Palapa – thatch made of woven, Mexican fan-palm leaves

Photography: Steven House

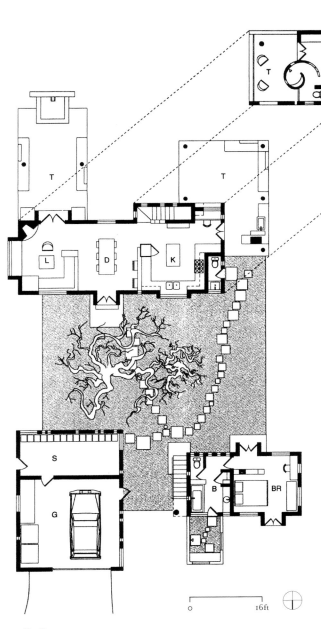

T – Terrace
L – Living
D – Dining
K – Kitchen
MB – Master Bedroom
BR – Bedroom
B – Bathroom
G – Garage
S – Storage

Alpert Residence

Jeffrey Gordon Smith Landscape Architects

Nine integral, colour concrete triangular monoliths were designed for this residential courtyard garden. The fountains were designed to be a passive water display during the day and a cityscape light show at night.

The black colour of the triangular concrete monoliths were embedded with plexi-glass triangles that are lit with fibre-optic strands. During the day, the effect is a beautiful, tranquil display of water sheering down each of the three sides of the nine monoliths.

At night, the courtyard becomes a mood-altering experience as the fibre-optic system changes slowly from one colour to another. The whole series of monoliths is flanked by timber bamboo, which echoes the vertical elements. The water travels down through the Mexican pebbles into a basin and is re-circulated back through the columns.

Photography: Elliot Johnson

HC House in Aroeira

Saraiva & Associados

Surrounded by forest, the HC House is located a few kilometres away from the Aroeira Golf Resort, the largest resort in the greater Lisbon area. Situated within a beautiful preservation area, the dominant green colour of the golfing green blends with the mature trees of the nearby pine forest.

One of the main concepts of this T-shaped, single-family house is its relationship between the interior and exterior that makes the best use of the garden and its surroundings. The living areas and bedrooms all share an expansive view of the outdoors through large glass façades. A rooftop terrace accessed from a stairway in the living room, allows privileged access to the view from above.

The architectural language is mainly minimalist, sober and transparent. This restrained style is demarcated through glazed orthogonal lines and is emphasised by its direct connection with the outdoors.

Photography: FG + SG Fotografia de Arquitectura

LOTE 173

LOTE 173

Campo de Golfe

Courtyard Townhouse

Arcod Architects

The owner asked for privacy and quiet despite a location on a main street in Tel Aviv and so this residence was created within a 'shell'.

The shell offers protection and shuts out the noise of the city. The house and garden are combined in a single unit within sloped, sealed walls. The resulting courtyard is a haven amidst the chaos and noisy environment.

Outdoor spaces consist of a sheltered courtyard with comfortable seating. Umbrellas protect against the searing midday sun. Landscaped garden spaces with shrubs and other plantings provide a soothing green respite.

Photography: Amit Geron

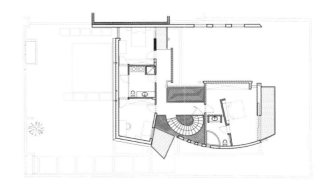

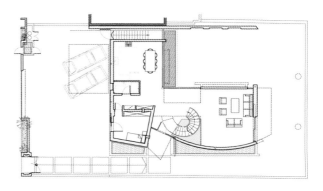

Slavin-Arnholz Residence

ROCK CREEK PARK, WASHINGTON D.C., USA

Travis Price Architects

This existing home is a small house with a slate roof built in the early 1900s in a Tudor cottage-style. The residence's area was virtually doubled by the addition of a four-level structure at the back. Large trees surround this very narrow site sloping into creek land.

The verticality of the structure and the trees were further enhanced by a series of outdoor terraces at each level culminating in a roof, surrounded by the park trees. The roof terrace is nearly 20 metres up in the air nestled among abutting oak trees that continue to soar another 10 metres or more. The roof access structure is the last set of steps wrapped in translucent fibreglass walls. The decks are recycled dock materials, the exterior skin in a green patina of copper. Glass railings and furniture are constructed out of climbing ropes.

The design merges with the adjacent parklands harmonising with the natural green colours.

Photography: Kenneth M. Wyner

Bonifields Residence

Jeffrey Gordon Smith Landscape Architecture

This mid-century modern home is in an older neighbourhood surrounded by hilltop vistas. The home's design brought the outdoors in, with every room having a door that opens to an outdoor space.

Three new patios were designed, each with its own individual planting style that could be viewed from the interior spaces. The first garden was designed with a native planting, the second with an Asian planting and the third designed for bird watching. On the front of the home, a huge expanse of glass brings the hilltop views indoors and opens onto the front balcony.

Below the balcony, the bocce ball courtyard is of decomposed granite. A native California and Mediterranean plant palette surrounds the court.

An ipe screen provides a privacy barrier from the street. The paver pathway from the ipe screen serves as a spirit walk, borrowing from a Japanese tradition, where a straight path jogs quickly to one side to let the evil spirit continue on the straight path. Exposed aggregate and buff-coloured concrete form a grid pattern on all of the main patios with Mexican pebbles as a ground cover in several areas.

Photography: Elliot Johnson

Rotenberg House

Minarc

This luxurious home is located on prime Malibu Beach ocean front property. An open plan, two-storey design accentuates the beach lifestyle.

The courtyard is situated at the front of the home and is often used as a play area for the children. Because the home is situated in an urban neighbourhood, bamboo plantings offer a degree of privacy from the neighbours. Pebble stones and grass heighten the feeling of cosiness.

A concrete path surrounded by pebble stones leads to a teak pivot door. A portion of the front elevation is clad with a teak trellis that provides privacy from the busy street and lets the light in. The outdoor spaces provide an oasis of calm and serenity in a busy, urban area.

Photography: Ralf Seeburger

Villa Room

This unique and energy efficient house has a number of added features, one being a weather station on the roof for measuring wind and sun. Connected to a central computer that controls the installation, air circulation, sun exposure, heating, cooling and maximising energy are all fully controlled.

All spaces are designed around the atrium which functions as a light court and brings the northern light into the house. A spacious outdoor wooden deck promotes indoor/outdoor harmony and allows optimal views of the surrounding nature.

Photography: Alessio Guarino, Rob 't Hart

Architectenbureau Paul de Ruiter B.V.

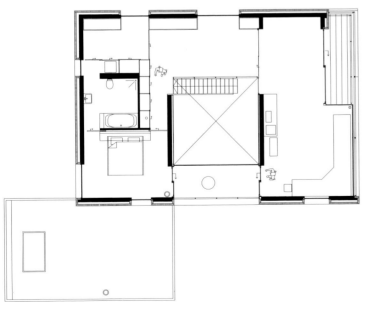

Casa Perdenal

Daniel Perez-Gil Arquitectos

Casa Pedernal's design scheme is focused on promoting an interior lifestyle around a central garden. The swimming pool forms a centrepiece and is designed as a grand canal where a large wall acts as a showcase for the water concept.

A large wooden deck is a focal point in the design scheme and provides the link between the outdoors with the indoors. A series of crystal lights at ground level provides a luminous incandescence at night.

Pedestrian access is via a path that separates the garden area, swimming pool and terrace from the house. The entire design concept is transparent and the outdoor areas are at one with the interior.

Photography: Hector Armando Herrera

Shalvoy Residence

Minarc

The owners of the Shalvoy Residence, a news writer and a lawyer, required an airy, open residence that embodies the casual beach atmosphere. Located on one of Manhattan Beach's walk streets on a narrow lot, it is within walking distance from California's Sandy Beach.

The exterior living spaces echo the interior, being very light and open. A courtyard extending outward from the kitchen allows for outdoor living. Large French windows that open fully from the kitchen area merge the indoors with the outdoors and emphasise the beachside California lifestyle.

Photography: Douglas Olson